AIRCRAFT

Coast Guard Rescue and Patrol Aircraft

Henry M. Holden

Enslow Publishers, Inc.

40 Industrial Road   PO Box 38
Box 398   Aldershot
Berkeley Heights, NJ 07922 Hants GU12 6BP
USA   UK

http://www.enslow.com

Library of Congress Cataloging-in-Publication Data

Holden, Henry M.
    Coast Guard rescue and patrol aircraft / Henry M. Holden.
        p. cm. — (Aircraft)
    Includes bibliographical references and index.
    ISBN 0-7660-1715-X
    1. United States. Coast Guard—Aviation—Juvenile literature. 2. United
States. Coast Guard—Search and rescue operations—Juvenile literature.
3. Reconnaissance aircraft—United States—Juvenile literature. 4. Aerial
observation (Military science)—United States—Juvenile literature. [1. United
States. Coast Guard—Aviation. 2. United States. Coast Guard—Search and
rescue operations. 3. Rescue work. 4. Airplanes, Military.] I. Title. II. Aircraft
(Berkeley Heights, N.J.)
    VG53 .H64 2002
    363.28'6'0973—dc21

                                                                    2001002070

Printed in the United States of America

10 9 8 7 6 5 4 3 2 1

To Our Readers: We have done our best to make sure all Internet addresses in this book were active and appropriate when we went to press. However, the author and the publisher have no control over and assume no liability for the material available on those Internet sites or on other Web sites they may link to. Any comments or suggestions can be sent by e-mail to comments@enslow.com or to the address on the back cover.

Photo Credits: © Corel Corporation, pp. 3, 11, 24, 31, 35; Henry M. Holden, p. 27; National Aeronautics and Space Administration, p. 21; U.S. Coast Guard, pp. 1, 4–5, 7, 9, 12, 13, 15, 16, 18, 19, 23, 25, 26, 28, 30, 32, 34, 36, 39, 41, 42, 43.

Cover Photo: U.S. Coast Guard

Contents

1 A Dolphin to the Rescue.................. 4

2 Aircraft and Equipment 11

3 Coast Guard Aircrews..... 24

4 Iceberg Alley 31

5 A Flight to Hawaii 35

Active Coast Guard Aircraft 41

Chapter Notes 44

Glossary 46

Further Reading and Internet Addresses 47

Index 48

CHAPTER 1

A Dolphin to the Rescue

HH-65 Dolphin helicopter

It was January 3, 1989. It was cold, and there was a low dark cloud cover. A heavy rain beat on the roof of the Coast Guard Air Station in Astoria, Oregon. It was not a good day for flying. The harsh blare of the search-and-rescue alarm had just sounded. The pilot and weapons systems officer of the Oregon National Guard had bailed out of their F-4 fighter jet over the Pacific Ocean. The water was very cold, and the F-4 crew could be in a lot of trouble.

The crew of a twin-engine HH-65 Dolphin helicopter would try to rescue the two injured men. The Dolphin carries two pilots, a flight mechanic, and a rescue swimmer. The copilot of the rescue helicopter, Lieutenant William Harper, performed the preflight checklist, a visual inspection of the helicopter. He looked for cracks or damage on the helicopter. He also checked the blades on the main and tail rotors for damage. Then the pilot, Lieutenant Commander William Peterson, started the engines.

The air station's HU-25 Guardian twin-engine jet would also join the search. The jet cannot pull survivors from the water. Its crew might spot them and drop a datum marker buoy. This buoy sends out an electronic signal that would lead the Dolphin to the site. A second Dolphin helicopter would follow as a backup.

The helicopter took off and headed toward the last reported location of the two men. There was heavy rain over the ocean and almost no visibility. Without warning, the helicopter broke out of the clouds. The pilot could see about a hundred feet above him and about a thousand feet around him. The sea had angry twenty-foot waves.

The Dolphin cannot land in the water. A rescue swimmer might have to jump into the ocean to help the injured men into a basket. The basket would then lift

The Coast Guard's HU-25 Guardian is used mostly for search and rescue and law enforcement missions.

the men into the helicopter. Peterson felt it was important to tell rescue swimmer Kelly Mogk the truth. "I hope we don't have to lower you. Depending on what we run into we might have to leave you for the other helicopter to pick up."[1] The small helicopter might be too crowded with the two F-4 crew members, who might be seriously injured.

The pilots soon spotted one person clinging to a raft. "It was pure luck that we found anyone," said Peterson.

The downed pilot of the F-4 was hanging on to the side of the raft. Every wave was breaking over his head. He could not pull himself into the raft. Peterson flew low enough to see the man's face and eyes. His skin was dark, his stare vacant. "He's dying. We've got to be quick," Peterson called to the crew.

Kelly Mogk—in her orange diving suit, flippers, mask, and snorkel—looked like a creature from another planet. With the helicopter in a hover about fifteen feet over the water, Mogk jumped from the aircraft. Fighting the twenty-foot waves, Mogk swam to the survivor.

"Hang on. The helicopter is here," she said.

He did not respond. She squeezed his hand. He could barely squeeze back. She knew he was dying. She *had* to save him.

Mogk looked underwater below the raft. She saw the problem. The pilot's parachute was open and full of water. It was dragging him down.

She got her knife out, took a deep breath, and dived under the raft. She was going to cut the parachute lines.

An HH-65 Dolphin helicopter demonstrates one rescue method using a ring to pick up a rescue swimmer. The flight mechanic operates the hoist that lifts the swimmer back onto the helicopter.

This was dangerous. Mogk could become entangled in the lines and drown.

Kelly Mogk's diving suit had sprung a leak. The icy water was now seeping into her diving suit. She was already starting to shiver. Soon she would begin to feel the numbing effects of the cold water.

Mogk worked for twenty minutes to free the pilot from his parachute. The flight mechanic then hoisted the pilot up to the helicopter. "In twelve years I've saved many people on hundreds of search-and-rescue cases," said Peterson, "but these were the worst conditions under which I've ever put a rescue swimmer down."[2]

The man had blue skin and nearly black lips. Peterson knew he was near death. He made a tough decision. Minutes lost pulling Kelly Mogk up may mean the survivor could die. "I think this guy is very close to being dead," he radioed to the other Dolphin. "I want you to pick up my swimmer."

Peterson passed his decision down to Mogk with hand signals. She watched the door close and the helicopter fly away.

Minutes later the second helicopter arrived on scene. It searched for the missing weapons officer. Unable to find him, the crew hoisted Mogk aboard and flew back to the air station.

The rescued pilot survived. For her heroism, Kelly Mogk, the first woman to qualify as a rescue swimmer in the Coast Guard, was awarded the Air Medal in January, 1989.[3]

CHAPTER 2

Aircraft and Equipment

The Coast Guard is a branch of the Department of Transportation. In time of war, it is part of the armed forces of the United States. Its mission is to rescue the victims of floods and storms, keep illegal drugs from coming into the United States, and help clean up oil spills. They use five different types of aircraft for these missions. There are more than two hundred aircraft in the Coast Guard fleet.[1]

All Coast Guard aircraft and ships are painted white with a red stripe. The coloration allows them to be seen in low-visibility conditions.

The cockpits of all Coast Guard aircraft are jam-packed with electronic equipment

Coast Guard personnel assist medical staff to transport an emergency medevac patient to the hospital. The HH-60 Jayhawk helicopter landed on the roof of the hospital.

such as radar and radios. They have buttons, switches, and control panels. All aircraft have the same basic flight instruments. An altimeter shows how high the aircraft is flying. An airspeed indicator, which works like a speedometer, shows how fast the aircraft is going. Each aircraft may also have other instruments and equipment, depending on its use.

HC-130 Hercules

The HC-130 Hercules is the Coast Guard's largest airplane. Its wingspan of over 132 feet is about the length of four school buses. It is almost 98 feet long and has a range of 5,178 miles. It can fly for up to fourteen hours and over six miles high. The Hercules flies at about 330 miles per hour.

The Hercules is a four-engine turboprop. A turboprop aircraft uses jet engines to turn the propellers. Each engine produces about 4,600 horsepower. (By comparison, a car engine has about 150 to 200 horsepower.) It carries two pilots and a flight crew of up to five, depending on its mission.

The HC-130 is used for several types of missions. It flies search-and-rescue (SAR) and law enforcement

The HC-130 Hercules is the largest airplane in the Coast Guard. It is used to perform search and rescue, law enforcement, marine environmental protection, and International Ice Patrol missions.

missions. It protects the ocean environment and looks for people trying to immigrate illegally. It also flies International Ice Patrol missions.

The Hercules cannot land on the water. As a rescue aircraft, it can drop flares, rafts, and food to people in the water. With skis on its landing gear, it can take off and land on snow.

≡ Environmental Protection and Law Enforcement

The Hercules can carry a team of about sixty people trained to fight oil spills. They take along special equipment, including a thirty-two-foot motor home. This is their mobile command post. It is rolled into the enormous back end of the HC-130 and flown to the disaster scene. The team carries a machine that can pump 1,800 gallons of oil a minute. It is used to pump oil from a leaking ship to another ship before it spills into the ocean. They also carry a 600-foot-long tube called a boom that unfolds on the water. It inflates and surrounds the oil spill, creating a barrier and keeping the oil from spreading.[2]

On law enforcement missions, the Hercules follows suspected drug-smuggling airplanes at high altitudes. It uses radar and forward-looking infrared sensors (FLIR). At night or in fog, a FLIR sensor can detect the heat from another airplane's engine. The heat is called the plane's heat signature, and the FLIR normally display this signature in black and white. Some infrared equipment

The huge Hercules aircraft contains room for lots of equipment. The large back of the aircraft opens, and personnel can roll in the cargo.

can detect a sixteen-inch-wide hotspot from 8,000 feet.[3] With a FLIR the Coast Guard can fly high above the suspected aircraft and not be seen.

≡ HU-25 Guardian

The HU-25 Guardian is a 56-foot-long twin-engine jet. It has a 54-foot wingspan. The Guardian is the fastest aircraft in the Coast Guard fleet. It has a top speed of over 500 miles per hour and a range of almost 2,000 miles. This is about the distance between Los Angeles,

The Coast Guard's HU-25 Guardian aircraft is a twin-engine jet.

California, and Chicago, Illinois. It can fly as high as 41,000 feet for almost six hours.

The Guardian is mainly used for search and rescue, law enforcement, and ocean environmental protection. On law enforcement missions, the HU-25 has a crew of four: a pilot, copilot, and two sensor system operators (SSO). The SSOs operate the search radar and the FLIR. This radar can detect smuggler airplanes up to 120 miles away. The Guardian will fly high above the suspect aircraft, where it will not be seen.

When flying oil spill missions, the HU-25 Guardian uses the same crew of four. The Guardian can fly to accident sites faster than the HC-130 and locate the spill. The SSOs operate the side-looking airborne radar (SLAR). SLAR works on a simple principle: Since oil calms the normal wave action on the ocean, the SLAR operator looks for areas of the sea without waves. This calm sea will be the location of the oil spill. Once the spill is located, the Guardian crew can determine how large it is and what kind of clean-up equipment is needed. Commander Tom Seckler, an HU-25 Guardian pilot, described oil spill missions this way: "You must fly nice long straight tracks. The SLAR is extremely sensitive to the motion of the aircraft. We fly at about eight thousand feet. From that altitude, we can detect oil spills to twenty-seven miles on either side of the aircraft."[4]

≡ HH-60 Jayhawk

The Coast Guard's HH-60 Jayhawk is the largest helicopter in its fleet. It is almost 65 feet long, about the length of two school buses. It carries a four-person crew: two pilots, a flight mechanic, and a rescue swimmer. It has one 54-foot main rotor with four whirling blades. Each blade is made of fiberglass, but the tip is covered with titanium. The blades are filled with nitrogen gas as a crack-detection device. If any nitrogen leaks, a detector senses this, which indicates a crack in the rotor blade. The Jayhawk flies at a maximum speed of about 200 miles per hour. It can fly for about five hours without refueling.

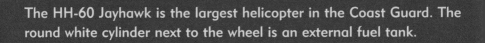

The HH-60 Jayhawk is the largest helicopter in the Coast Guard. The round white cylinder next to the wheel is an external fuel tank.

Models with external fuel tanks can go without refueling for seven hours.

Search-and-Rescue Mission

"When we get a Mayday call that a boat is in trouble, we have to move fast," said Lieutenant Jeff McCullars, a Coast Guard Jayhawk pilot. "We know that lives depend on how fast we get to the scene."[5]

The pilots have an idea of the boat's location from the radio transmission. They program this information into a computer, which will predict the tides and winds in the area. The computer will also tell them where the boat has most likely drifted because of the tides and winds. "We then take this information and program it into the flight computer on the helicopter," said McCullars.

The Jayhawk's flight computer can be programmed to fly the helicopter. This means the helicopter can operate without a pilot's hands on the controls. The flight computer can also be used as an autopilot. When a destination is input, it sets a course for the helicopter to fly.

"The flight computer can fly us right down to the wave tops so that the rescue swimmer can jump into

An HH-60 Jayhawk helicopter is about to pick up a rescue swimmer. The downwash from the rotor blades makes this a difficult task.

the water," said McCullars. "We don't have to touch the controls. The computer flies into a nice stable hover."[6]

Coast Guard pilots use the Global Positioning System (GPS) to help navigate. The GPS uses signals from three or four of the 24 satellites that are 12,500 miles out in space. It can figure out exactly where the helicopter is. This helps guide the helicopter to within a few feet of the boat.

During a search-and-rescue mission, the Jayhawk will fly at about 100 miles per hour. This way the pilots have a chance to look for small boats in the vast ocean. If it flies too fast, the waves rush by and it is harder to spot a small boat or people in the water. With its additional external fuel tanks, the Jayhawk can travel about 700 miles—instead of 550 miles—before it needs refueling.

Once the sinking boat has been located, the people will be lifted aboard the helicopter in a basket. This basket is attached to a rescue hoist that can lift up to 600 pounds.

≡ Seeing in the Dark

At night, the Jayhawk crew wears alien-looking night-vision goggles to help them look for victims. Night-vision goggles intensify the light from the moon, stars, and ground 2,000 to 3,500 times.[7] Even on the darkest night, there is enough light in the sky to allow pilots using night-vision goggles to see. The pilot does not see as if it were daylight: Everything shows up in pale shades of green.

Night-vision goggles fit over the flight helmet and are worn by the flight crew when they are searching for someone at night. The person sees everything in a green glow like the color in this photo.

≡ HH-65 Dolphin

The HH-65 Dolphin helicopter is smaller than the Jayhawk. The twin-engine Dolphin flies the same missions as the Jayhawk, but it is used for shorter-range flights of about 300 miles. It is almost 45 feet long and has a 39-foot rotor blade. Its top speed is about 190 miles per hour. It can fly for about three or four hours before refueling. It carries a four-person crew: two pilots, a flight mechanic, and a rescue swimmer.

Like the Jayhawk, the Dolphin has an automatic flight control system and a GPS. It also has an emergency flotation system. This is used only if the helicopter has to make an emergency landing in the water. The Jayhawk does not have this because it is too heavy.

The Dolphin and the Jayhawk both have a 3.5-million-candlepower Nightsun searchlight. The searchlight can turn darkness into daylight and is used for spotting people at night.

≡ MH-90 Power Enforcer

The MH-90 Power Enforcer helicopter is the latest Coast Guard weapon against the war on drugs. Smaller than the Dolphin, it can land on the deck of any large Coast Guard ship. (The Dolphin and Jayhawk can land on only the largest cutters.) This twin-engine helicopter has a four-blade main rotor that is 36 feet long. It can cruise at about 195 miles per hour. It has two pilots and one crew member.

The Enforcer helicopter is specifically designed to chase drug-smuggling boats.

The MH-90 helicopter has weather radar that keeps the pilots informed of wild storms ahead. The FLIR, which can detect objects in the dark, can videotape drug-smuggling boats.

The MH-90 also carries a 7.62-mm swivel-mounted machine gun and a laser-sighted .50-caliber rifle. The crew member is an expert sharpshooter and is responsible for firing these guns. The machine gun is used to fire warning shots across the bow of a fleeing smuggler's boat. The .50-caliber rifle will shoot rubber bullets at the engine to stop it. These guns are used only if the smugglers fire upon the helicopter first.

CHAPTER 3

Coast Guard Aircrews

There are three ways to become a Coast Guard pilot. The first is to be a pilot in other military services and transfer into the Coast Guard. The second is to attend the U.S. Coast Guard Academy and request pilot training after graduation. The third is through officer candidate school (OCS). Once a person completes OCS, he or she can apply to flight school.

Pilot Training

The U.S. Navy conducts pilot training for the Coast Guard. It takes a year to complete this training, which consists of ground school and flight training. In ground school, students learn about weather and the physics of flight.

Rick Kepley does a preflight check on a Dolphin helicopter. The preflight is to make sure the helicopter is safe to fly.

Actual flight training starts with a series of familiarization flights called Fams. During Fam 1, the instructor flies the plane. He allows the student to take the controls, though, to get the feel of the airplane.

On Fam 2, the student takes off. On Fam 3, the student lands the airplane. By Fam 13, the student is ready for his check ride, during which the student shows the instructor everything he has learned. If he passes, he will fly solo on Fam 14.

The student also learns instrument flying on simulators. The inside of some simulators look like the

Here is a look inside the cockpit of the Coast Guard's HH-65 Dolphin helicopter as it prepares to land on the back of a Coast Guard ship. Pilots that fly Coast Guard aircraft first need to train with the U.S. Navy for one year.

inside of an airplane or helicopter. The pilot has a large screen in front of him, the kind found in an arcade game. Simulators allow pilots to experience flying situations without ever leaving the ground. After practicing instrument flying in a simulator, the student will fly on instruments in real aircraft.[1]

During pilot training the students will fly fixed-wing aircraft and helicopters. Upon successful completion of pilot training, the officer will be a U.S. Coast Guard pilot.

After graduation, the new pilot will take advanced flight training in one type of aircraft: helicopters, jets, or turboprops. Every pilot can request which aircraft he or she would like to fly. The selection process involves the pilot's grades, his or her flying skills, and the difficulty of the aircraft. For example, not every pilot can go to advanced helicopter training. Only the best basic helicopter pilots are picked for this training.

Lieutenant Jeff McCullars, an HH-60 Jayhawk pilot, knows that flying involves teamwork.

"You need to know math, science, English, and play team sports. Flying involves teamwork. You also need good verbal communications skills," said Lieutenant Jeff McCullars.[2]

Rescue Swimmers

Rescue swimmers, also known as aviation survival technicians (ASTs), jump into the water from helicopters to help rescue people. They are highly trained and work in the toughest physical conditions imaginable: They plunge into ice-cold water, often fighting huge waves and swift currents. They work on the edge of danger, where mistakes can cost lives.

There are 36,000 men and women in the Coast Guard, but only 306 men and 2 women are rescue swimmers. In the fifteen years they have been doing this work, rescue swimmers have helped rescue almost five thousand people. They have never lost a swimmer.[3]

The training is tough. "It takes a special kind of person to do this job," said Tristan Heaton, an instructor. "We deal constantly with the possibility of injury. There is also the chance we may be left behind on the high seas.

"We send our guys in harm's way all the time. But it is okay for a rescue swimmer to say no to the mission," said Heaton. It is easy to jump into the water and escape by the seat of your pants. It takes a more mature person to say no if it is too dangerous, he says.

"No one gives you this job," said one rescue swimmer. "You have to work for it. You have to have a calling to do this kind of work."[4]

During a military training session, U.S. Marines leap from an HH-60 Jayhawk.

Rescue Swimmer Training

All ASTs attend a sixteen-week "A" School training at Air Station Elizabeth City, North Carolina. The training is intense. It separates the weak from the dedicated. It takes exceptional motivation to make it through "A" School. Half of the applicants do not complete the training.

After intense morning physical training, students put in three to four hours of classroom work. They spend afternoons training on cliff rescues and climbing up wet rocks. While fighting high waves in the rough seas from twenty-man rafts, they sometimes vomit.

Following "A" School there is a four-week Navy Rescue Swimmer School in Pensacola, Florida. ASTs also receive training as emergency medical technicians. After this training, they go to Advanced Rescue Swimmer School. They learn to conduct rescues in bad weather and heavy surf conditions, including those caused by hurricanes. They train at Cape Disappointment, Oregon. Cape D, as it is called, is known for its cold water, big swells, pounding surf, steep wet cliffs, swift currents, and deep caves.

After the ASTs graduate, they face a continuing series of tests. Each month all ASTs take a physical training test. They have to do sit-ups, push-ups, pull-ups, and underwater swims. If they fail the tests, they are immediately suspended from rescue swimmer duty. This can be permanent unless they pass the tests again.

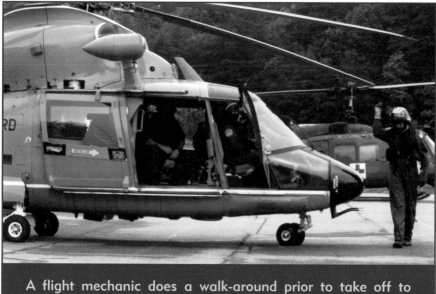

A flight mechanic does a walk-around prior to take off to make sure there is no debris that could fly up into the engines and damage the helicopter.

≡ Flight Mechanic

The flight mechanic, or aviation maintenance technician, is responsible for keeping the aircraft working properly. He must see that it is safe to fly and repair it when needed.

When the rescue swimmer is in the water, the flight mechanic is responsible for operating the hoist. He also gives directions to the pilot, who cannot see directly beneath the aircraft. If the hoist cable becomes entangled in the boat's equipment, the helicopter could be pulled out of the sky and into the water.

CHAPTER 4

Iceberg Alley

On the night of April 14, 1912, the largest ship afloat, the RMS *Titanic*, was moving swiftly through icy waters. It was passing over the Grand Banks area of the North Atlantic Ocean, about 800 miles from New York. Two men in the crow's nest, a wire cage 95 feet up on the mast, sounded the alarm. *Iceberg ahead!* The helmsman steering the ship tried to turn the ship away from the huge mountain of ice. It was too late. Everyone said the RMS *Titanic* was unsinkable, but the ship collided with the iceberg and sank in less than three hours. More than 1,500 people died. The public was shocked and angry. They wanted it never to happen again.

The United States and other countries with large shipping fleets set up the International Ice Patrol. Cutters were sent to patrol the Grand Banks to look for icebergs. Cutters are large fast ships capable of sailing in rough water.

Iceberg Patrol

Today, the icy Grand Banks area is called Iceberg Alley. It is approximately 500,000 square miles. Most of the icebergs that reach Iceberg Alley come from glaciers in western Greenland. About 10,000 to 15,000 form each year in this area. Only about 200 make it to Iceberg Alley.

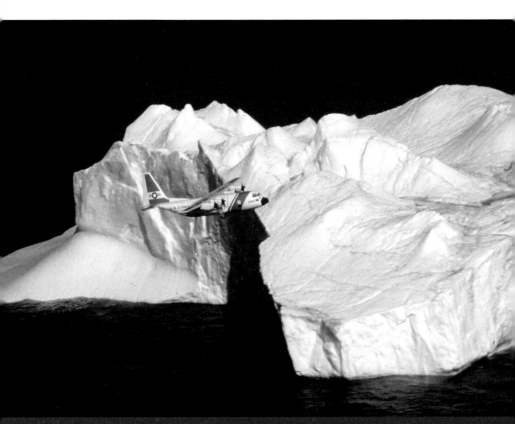

Even the biggest airplane in the Coast Guard, the HC-130, seems small next to this giant iceberg. Service with the International Ice Patrol is one of the many operations of the HC-130 Hercules.

They range in size from twenty-foot "growlers" to multibillion pound icebergs the size of aircraft carriers.[1]

The primary mission of the Coast Guard iceberg patrol is to search for and map ice floating near Iceberg Alley. The combination of icebergs, fog, severe storms, and busy Atlantic shipping lanes makes this area dangerous to sail. Icebergs are dangerous when they float into shipping lanes. The Coast Guard must warn ships of any dangerous icebergs in their path. Since the International Ice Patrol began its work, an iceberg has not sunk a single ship.

Today, Coast Guard HC-130 aircraft have replaced the cutters on ice patrol. They can cover more distance and are faster than the cutters. The HC-130 is jam-packed with electronic equipment. Its crew searches the sea for icebergs with binoculars or night-vision goggles, although dense fog sometimes obscures their vision. They also operate search radar, FLIR, and SLAR. With this equipment, they can detect distant icebergs.

The Coast Guard makes about sixty-five flights during the iceberg season, which runs from February to July.[2] Lieutenant Commander Alan Summy said that they can fly six hours, never see the surface of the ocean, yet find a number of icebergs with their SLAR.[3] SLAR detects icebergs as large areas of flat space surrounded by waves. Computers track the direction in which the icebergs float.

Small icebergs do not usually damage big ships. In the past, the Coast Guard has tried to break up large icebergs. They have used torpedoes, underwater bombs, and

A Coast Guard aircrew member in the back of an HC-130 Hercules prepares to drop a dye marker on an iceberg in the North Atlantic during an International Ice Patrol. Although it is hard to see, he has a safety harness on that keeps him from falling out. The wire from his helmet is the radio connection to the cockpit.

explosive charges. Since some icebergs are so large, these methods do not work.

To plant explosives, sailors had to climb onto the icebergs, which was dangerous. It would take about 1,900 tons of TNT to break up an average-sized iceberg. If they wanted to melt such an iceberg, it would take the heat of about 2.4 million gallons of burning gasoline.[4] These methods are too dangerous and expensive.

Instead, guardsmen use the electronic equipment on the aircraft to warn ships of icebergs in their path. At the end of each flight, the data is relayed to computers on land. Twice a day, the computerized positions of all known icebergs are broadcast to ships in the area.[5]

Now let us travel to the warm waters of the Pacific Ocean. A pilot and his passenger are in danger.

CHAPTER 5

A Flight to Hawaii

*T*he trouble started halfway over the ocean, between California and Hawaii. An engine oil low-pressure light signaled a warning. The pilot of the single-engine Piper airplane would have to crash-land in the ocean if the engine stopped.

The pilot radioed a Mayday call. The Coast Guard heard it and immediately launched an HC-130 Hercules from its air station in Barbers Point, Hawaii.

About three hours later, the pilot of the Piper and his passenger saw the HC-130. The pilot radioed the HC-130 and said that the Piper's oil pressure was still dropping.

The pilot had two choices. He could fly toward the nearest ship that could rescue

A Coast Guard HC-130, like the one shown here, took off from Hawaii on a mission to help the downed pilots.

them and make an emergency water landing in daylight. This is usually very risky, because the plane could break up when it hit the water. He could also try to make it to Hawaii, but it would be dark by the time they got there. They were more than a thousand miles away. The pilot was hoping the Piper could make it to Hawaii.

Later, by the time the sun had set, the Piper and its HC-130 escort had flown almost two hundred miles together. A brilliant moon made visibility excellent. That was about to change.

The planes flew into a rainstorm and lost sight of each other. Then the Piper's engine failed. The pilot radioed for help. "Hey, guys, it doesn't look like we'll make it," he said.

"You could hear it in his voice. He was very nervous," said Lieutenant Matthew Reid, the HC-130's aircraft commander.[1]

≡ Runway in the Sea

The Coast Guard plane had been flying at 7,000 feet—1,000 feet above the Piper. When the pilot said his engine had failed, Reid threw the Hercules into a sharp, diving turn. He dropped down below the Piper and raced ahead of it.

Reid's plan was to use flares to light up a "runway in the sea" for the pilot. Reid had told the pilot to follow them so that his airplane would be parallel to the ocean's ten-foot waves when he hit the water. However, there was a problem. In the rainstorm the HC-130 crew could not see if the Piper was behind them.

In the back of the HC-130, crew members began dropping flares, which burn for up to sixty minutes. They also dropped a datum marker buoy, which transmits a radio signal. The buoy would mark the approximate location of where the Piper was going down.

The Piper's radio stopped about fifteen seconds after its engine quit. Fortunately, before his radio went out, the pilot heard the message from the HC-130.

As the Piper came out of the clouds, the pilot saw the line of flares lighting up the ocean. The flares provided a frame of reference to judge the plane's altitude. It also allowed the pilot to see how the waves were breaking. Reid's runway in the sea was working, but the Piper was losing altitude fast. The two men braced for the impact.

"A few seconds later we heard no noise in the background. We knew he had gone into the water," said Reid.

After the crash, the two men climbed out of the plane and onto one of the wings. The pilot threw the Piper's life raft into the water, but it did not inflate.

The plane sank within minutes. The pilot and his passenger jumped off the wing into the ocean. In the darkness and confusion, the life raft disappeared. Worse yet, the emergency radio beacon was on it.

The HC-130 had life rafts it could drop to the pilot and his passenger—if they could spot them.

The crew continued searching for two more hours. However, in the rainstorm, there was little visibility. By 9:30 P.M. the Coast Guard plane was running low on fuel. Reluctantly, Reid turned his aircraft toward Barbers Point. The two men were alone in their struggle against the sea, if they were still alive.

"It was an extremely difficult decision," Reid said.

≡ Alone in the Ocean

The pilot and his passenger heard the HC-130 flying its search patterns overhead. "We didn't know they'd lost us," the pilot said. "At one point, it came right at us. We thought they had us sighted. Then they turned away. After that, they did not come back."

Back in Hawaii, the Coast Guard ordered the closest Coast Guard cutter, *Kiska*, to the crash area. A second HC-130 also headed for the scene.

With the *Kiska* still three hundred miles from the crash area, the Coast Guard requested assistance from ships that were near where the Piper had gone down. The freighter *Nyon* was seventy miles from the downed Piper.

The second search plane arrived at the crash area at 12:30 A.M. It began looking for the survivors. The rainstorm had ended. The moon was providing good nighttime visibility.

"When you're looking for two people out on the open ocean at night, it is difficult. With the seas up about ten feet, it is very hard to find somebody," said Captain Roger Whorton, the second HC-130's aircraft commander.

≡ Rescue at Sea

Ten minutes into the search, Shane Reese, a crew member on the HC-130, spotted two dim lights through his night-vision goggles.

The Coast Guard cutter *Kiska* was sent to the crash area. It would help in the rescue mission.

"Without the night-vision goggles, it would have been impossible to see the lights," said Reese. "We went down as low as we could, but we still couldn't tell what we were looking at. We dropped flares and a datum marker buoy, and circled around until the *Nyon* arrived.

"We thought if it was a person, they'd be waving the lights. They looked like they weren't moving," Reese said.

The *Nyon* arrived at 3:15 A.M., and the HC-130 guided the ship to the dim lights.

"We were all listening to the radio," Reese said. "The *Nyon*'s captain said they heard somebody screaming. We felt great."

The two lights Reese had spotted were two small personal marker lights attached to the survivors' life jackets. The lights had saved their lives.

By 4:50 A.M. both men were safely aboard the *Kiska*. The pilot and his passenger were exhausted and dehydrated. Their eyes were red and swollen from prolonged exposure to the salt water. "We owe our lives to these fellows," the pilot told a group of reporters on shore. "We are very grateful."

The men and women of Coast Guard aviation are highly trained and motivated professionals. They use the latest aircraft and equipment. They are committed to saving lives—even, if necessary, risking their own lives so that others may live.

Active Coast Guard Aircraft

HH-60 Jayhawk Medium-Range Recovery Helicopter

Length—64 feet 10 inches

Height—16 feet 10 inches

Rotor blade length—54 feet

Fuel tank capacity—950 gallons

Maximum speed—207 miles per hour

Cruising speed—about 160 miles per hour

Crew—4

Endurance—about 7 hours

Range—about 800 miles

Service ceiling (altitude for best aircraft performance)—about 5,000 feet

Cargo sling capacity—6,000 pounds

Rescue hoist capacity—600 pounds

Engines—2

HH-60 Jayhawk

HC-130 Hercules Long-Range Surveillance Aircraft

Length—97 feet 9 inches

Height—38 feet 3 inches

Wingspan—132 feet 7 inches

Fuel tank capacity—about 9,250 gallons

Maximum speed—about 380 miles per hour

Cruising speed—about 330 miles per hour

Crew—about 7, depending on use

Endurance—about 14 hours

Range—over 5,000 miles

Service ceiling—33,000 feet

Engines—4

HC-130 Hercules

HU-25 Guardian Medium-Range Jet Surveillance Aircraft

Length—56 feet

Height—18 feet

Wingspan—54 feet

Fuel tank capacity—about 1,500 gallons

Maximum speed—517 miles per hour

Cruising speed—about 470 miles per hour

Crew—5

Endurance—about 5–6 hours

Range—about 2,232 miles

Service ceiling—41,000 feet

Engines—2

HU-25 Guardian

HH-65 Dolphin Short-Range Recovery Helicopter

Length—44 feet 5 inches
Height—13 feet
Rotor blade length—39 feet
Fuel tank capacity—280 gallons
Maximum speed—190 miles per hour
Cruising speed—about 140 miles per hour
Crew—4
Endurance—about 3.5 hours
Range—about 340 miles
Service ceiling—7,500 feet
Cargo sling capacity—2,000 pounds
Rescue hoist capacity—600 pounds
Engines—2

HH-65 Dolphin

MH-90 Power Enforcer

Length—42 feet 8 inches
Height—11 feet 6 inches
Rotor blade length—36 feet
Maximum speed—196 miles per hour
Crew—3
Range—600 miles
Engines—2

MH-90 Enforcer

Chapter Notes

Chapter 1. A Dolphin to the Rescue

1. Samuel A. Schreiner, *Mayday! Mayday!: The Most Exciting Missions of Rescue, Interdiction, and Combat in the 200-year Annals of the U.S. Coast Guard* (New York: Donald I. Fine, 1990), p. 22.

2. Ibid., p. 17.

3. U.S. Coast Guard, *U.S. Coast Guard Firsts, Lasts, and Record-Setting Achievements in Search and Rescue*, n.d. <http://www.uscg.mil/hq/g-cp/history/FirstsIndex.html> (April 5, 2001).

Chapter 2. Aircraft and Equipment

1. United States Department of Transportation, *U.S. Coast Guard*, March 15, 2001, <http://www.uscg.mil> (April 5, 2001).

2. Arthur Pearcy, *A History of U.S. Coast Guard* (Annapolis, Md.: Naval Institute Press, 1989), p. 141.

3. Paul Proctor, "Fire-Fighting Fleet Stretched to Limit as U.S. West Burns," *Aviation Week & Space Technology*, August 21, 2000, p. 38.

4. Robert Dorr, *U.S. Coast Guard Aviation* (Osceola, Wisc.: MBI Publishing Company, 1999), p. 120.

5. Author interview with Lieutenant Jeff McCullars, July 30, 1999.

6. Ibid.

7. U.S. Army, *Night Flight Techniques and Procedures*, Publication number TCI-204, December 1988, pp. 2–7.

Chapter 3. Coast Guard Aircrews

1. David M. Werner, "Oh, To Solo! A Student's Journal," *Naval Aviation News*, May/June 1998, p. 17.

2. Author interview with Lieutenant Jeff McCullars, July 30, 1999.

3. *ABC World News*, August 18, 2000.

4. Ibid.

Chapter 4. Iceberg Alley

1. Arthur Pearcy, *A History of U.S. Coast Guard* (Annapolis, Md.: Naval Institute Press, 1989), p. 142.

2. United States Department of Transportation, *U.S. Coast Guard*, "Frequently Asked Questions," March 15, 2001, <http://www.uscg.mil/faqs.html> (April 5, 2001).

3. Alan Summy, "Maritime Hazards: International Ice Patrol Promotes Safer Navigation," *AMVER Bulletin 1-94*, p. 15.

4. *International Ice Patrol (IIP)*, "Frequently Asked Questions," <http://www.uscg.mil/lantarea/iip/home.html> (April 5, 2001).

5. Summy, p. 15.

Chapter 5. A Flight to Hawaii

1. All quotes in this chapter are from Eric Hedaa, "The Longest Night," *Coast Guard Magazine Online*, April 2000, <http://www.uscg.mil/hq/g-cp/cb/May2000/contents.html> (April 6, 2001).

Air Medal—A medal awarded to aircrew members for bravery.

air station—Any small airport used by the Coast Guard.

boom—An inflatable barrier used to contain an oil spill.

cutter—Any of the large ships used by the Coast Guard.

datum marker buoy—A device that floats in the ocean and sends out a radio signal indicating its location.

flight mechanic—The person responsible for the proper mechanical function of an aircraft.

FLIR—Forward-looking infrared sensor. FLIR detects the heat from an aircraft's body and engine and displays it on a monitor similar to a television screen.

heat signature—The image on an infrared sensor screen produced by an aircraft's engine.

hover—To stay in the air without moving in any direction.

main rotor—The large rotor on top of a helicopter that lifts it into the air.

Mayday—An emergency call from a ship or an airplane.

medevac—Medical evacuation.

Nightsun—A 30-million-candlepower searchlight.

rescue swimmer—A trained emergency medical technician and swimmer who jumps into the water to rescue people.

SAR—Search and rescue. A mission in which the Coast Guard searches for and rescues people lost or adrift in the ocean or some remote location.

SLAR—Side-looking airborne radar. SLAR detects large areas of flat space on the ocean that indicate the presence of icebergs or oil spills.

tail rotor—A small rotor on the tail of most helicopters that keeps the body from spinning around.

turboprop—An airplane that uses propellers with a jet engine.

Further Reading

Books

Barrett, Thomas Beard. *Wonderful Flying Machines: A History of U.S. Coast Guard Helicopters.* Annapolis, Md.: Naval Institute Press, 1996.

Dorr, Robert. *U.S. Coast Guard Aviation.* Osceola, Wisc.: MBI Publishing Company, 1992.

Pearcy, Arthur. *A History of U.S. Coast Guard.* Annapolis, Md.: Naval Institute Press, 1989.

Internet Addresses

Black Hawk Publishing. *Women in Aviation.* "Resource Center." © 2001. <http://www.women-in-aviation.com>.

National Aeronautics and Space Administration. *Off to a Flying Start.* "Introduction to Flight." December 12, 1999. <http://ltp.larc.nasa.gov/flyingstart>.

Smithsonian National Air and Space Museum. © 1994–2001. <http://www.nasm.edu>.

United States Department of Transportation. *U.S. Coast Guard.* March 15, 2001. <http://www.uscg.mil>.

A
Air Medal, 10
airspeed indicator, 12
air station, 5, 6, 10, 29, 35
altimeter, 12
aviation maintenance technician.
See flight mechanic.
aviation survival technicians
(ASTs), 27–28, 29. See also
rescue swimmer.

B
boom, 14

C
Cape Disappointment (Oregon), 29
cutter, 32

D
datum marker buoy, 6, 40

E
emergency flotation system, 22

F
familiarization flights, 25
F-4 fighter jet, 6
flight computer, 19–20
flight mechanic, 6, 10, 17, 30
forward-looking infrared sensors
(FLIR) 14–15, 16, 23, 33

G
Global Positioning System (GPS), 20

H
Harper, William, 6
HC-130 Hercules, 12–14, 33, 36,
37–40, 42
Heaton, Tristan, 28
heat signature, 14
HH-60 Jayhawk, 17–20, 22, 41
HH-65 Dolphin, 6, 8, 22, 43
hover, 8, 20
HU-25 Guardian, 6, 15–17, 42

I
Iceberg Alley, 32–33
International Ice Patrol, 14, 32–33

K
Kiska, 38, 40

M
main rotor, 17, 22
McCullars, Jeff, 18, 27
MH-90 Power Enforcer, 22–23, 43
Mogk, Kelly, 8, 10

N
Nightsun, 22
night-vision goggles, 20, 40
Nyon, 39, 40

O
officer candidate school (OCS), 24

P
Peterson, William, 6, 10
pilot training, 24–27
Piper, 35–36, 37–38, 39

R
Reese, Shane, 39–40
Reid, Matthew, 36, 37–38
rescue hoist, 20
rescue swimmer, 6, 8, 10, 17,
27–28, 29, 30
RMS Titanic, 31

S
search-and-rescue alarm, 5
search-and-rescue mission (SAR), 13
Seckler, Tom, 17
sensor system operator (SSO), 16
side-looking airborne radar
(SLAR), 17, 33
simulators, 25–26
Summy, Alan, 33

T
tail rotor, 6
turboprop, 13

U
U.S. Coast Guard, 5, 10, 11–20,
22, 23–30, 33–34, 35–40
U.S. Coast Guard Academy, 24

W
Whorton, Roger, 39